SOULSCAPES

SOULSCAPES

poems by

LEE WOODMAN

SHANTI ARTS PUBLISHING

BRUNSWICK, MAINE

Soulscapes

Published by Shanti Arts Publishing

Designed by Shanti Arts Designs

Cover image: Jamo Images / stock.adobe.com

Shanti Arts LLC
193 Hillside Road
Brunswick, Maine 04011
shantiarts.com

Printed in the United States of America

ISBN: 978-1-962082-20-4 (softcover)

Library of Congress Control Number: 2023950771

For my sisters,
Deborah Coleman, who died in August 2022, and
Jane Cohen, who was heroic in her care.

Other Titles
by Lee Woodman

Homescapes
(Finishing Line Press)

Mindscapes
(Poets' Choice Publishing)

Lifescapes
(Kelsay Books)

Artscapes
(Shanti Arts Publishing)

Contents

Acknowledgments

The author extends great appreciation to the editors and publishers of the following publications in which versions of the following poems have appeared:

The Atlantic Review: "Postcards Way Over the Edge"

Carvezine: "Orca Ode"

The Ekphrastic Review: "The Healer" and "The Time-Markers"

The Hill Rag: "What to Expect at Congressional Cemetery"

Homescapes (Finishing Line Press): "Benumbed"; "Climbing the Rohtang Pass"; and "Trees Have Longer Lives"

Lifescapes (Kelsay Books): "Spirits" and "What to Expect at Congressional Cemetery"

Mindscapes (Poet's Choice Publishing): "A Child Asks" and "Reconsidering the Moon"

Thanks

I am grateful to the people who made this book possible ..

... my sister and first reader, novelist Betsy Woodman, who makes me jump higher and keeps me laughing;

... my master poets, critics and publishers: Emily Holland, Zeina Azzam, Grace Cavalieri, the late Chris Bursk, Sue Ellen Thompson, Richard Blanco, Alexandra Oliver, Lorette Luzajic, Jane Rosenberg LaForge, Sparrow, Richard Harteis, Leah Maines, Karen Kelsay, Claudia Gary, and Christine Cote;

... writers from the priceless Monday group, who kindly welcomed a poet among novelists: Elizabeth Berg, Mary Mitchell, Donna Stein, and Betsy Woodman;

... my reader and archivist, Bill Kircher, tarot guru, Tim Boyd, and marketing coach, Brian Feinblum;

... my cherished friends, and supporters: Craig Kraft, Virginia Rice, Sarah Toth, Randy Wynn, Julianna Jacobson, Pete Chauvette, Susan Clampitt, Jeremy Waletzky, Stephanie Cotsirilos, Madeleine Jacobs, and Marjorie Share;

... the talented women who made reading and writing so healing during the pandemic and will do so into the future: Dawn Raffel, Jill Smolove, Jane Rosenberg LaForge, Donna Stein, Betsy Woodman, Laura Weiss, Joanna Laufer, Ronna Weinberg, Pamela Walker, and Ellen Prentiss Campbell;

... the magical visionaries at the Writer's Hotel and *The New Guard* literary review: founding editor, Shanna McNair, and consulting editor, Scott Wolven;

... my generous instructors from the Writer's Center in Bethesda, Maryland: Judith Harris, Meg Eden, the late Nan Fry, Claudia Gary; and

... special gratitude for the artistry and support of Christine Cote at Shanti Arts.

—Lee Woodman

Thanks to adventuresome parents and a rich and tapestried childhood in France, India, and the United States, I was introduced to many ways of looking at the world. As a poet, wanderer, and wonderer, I try through my work to make sense of the universe. I call this volume *Soulscapes*—a journey toward connection and meaning through imagery and words.

Spiritually, I would call myself a seeker who admits, discovers, and ponders all gods. I learned growing up to be open to all aspects of faith: Hindu, Muslim, Jain, Buddhist, Christian, Jewish, Native American, and worldwide tribal beliefs. But perhaps my real religion is Education and Exploration.

I've steeped myself in research about many other areas of spiritual belief and practice: origin stories, spirit animals, tarot, witchcraft, the occult, past lives, lucid dreaming. Being both a rational skeptic and a believer in things unexplainable by logic, poetry seems the perfect way to explore and love both the scientific fact-based world and the magical, mysterious unknown.

Perhaps I see all beings as one with nature in the universe. Why would we be apart? And what else is out there in the far reaches of space? With recent developments never thought imaginable, like the James Webb Telescope, and the Chandra X-Ray Observatory, we are compelled to open our eyes to new visions of the universe—the galaxies "beyond."

I invite you to take this journey with me through *Soulscapes*, an exploration of the way we reach for godliness or soul in our lives and relations. May you consider and delight, as I have, in other ways of knowing.

—Lee Woodman

A Child Asks

What is God?

I think, not darkly,
God is death.
If ashes are ashes
and dust is dust,

I go underground and rest.
There I am fertilized

by loam and water,
beckoned by life-to-be.

When ready, I push up and
bloom color,

never knowing the hue.
I answer

the child who instinctively
knows azure is azure,

scarlet is scarlet, and
God is in the flower.

Bodhisattva of Compassion

In March 1959, after years of threats from China, His Holiness
the Dalai Lama crossed the Himalayas on foot in the freezing
night with a small retinue: his mother, sister, senior advisors,
and small children, all carrying babies.

Palms up, arms outstretched, we walk slowly
toward Him. Our private audience, June 1959.
Draped over Dad's forearms, a white silk scarf.

He transfers the khata to the Dalai Lama's arms;
I fix on the Leader's brown body, loose garnet robe,
smallpox vaccination, thick-framed black eyeglasses.

He asks about my father's religion, his work,
why he is in India. Sonam Topgai, interpreter, helps
Dad comprehend His Holiness's escape from Tibet.

Topgai leads us to the encampment by the river—
no beds, heat from small charcoal fires and twigs,
a ball of fried dough twice a day, tin cups of tea.

My father asks the Dalai Lama's sister and
her helpers, "What do the children need?"
They don't say food, clothes, blankets, or water,

only, "Could you send us a teacher?"

Much is lost from my memory of the audience
at that young age; I can't picture the compound,
I wonder if we removed our shoes.

Yet much stays indelible—the mystical walk
toward Him, the sparkle in his dark pupils,
the tinkling of his voice, his motion

to his assistant to bring back the khata.
His Holiness drapes it over Dad's arms
for our return—a gesture of protection.

Sweet silence—
No words, a sole beatific smile.
A child knows transcendence.

ts of the Dead

—inspired by Marvin Cone's *The Appointed Room*

We can make ourselves visible through the wall now,
    the movers have removed the furniture, loaded the truck

The bedroom, with doors on three sides, is empty,
    no non-believers sleep here anymore

Like parchment phantoms, we break through
    the wallpaper to breathe and tell our histories

All three doors are open, yet shadows cast do not correspond
    with multiple light sources

Splashes of brightness throw attention to groups
    of our faces, neck to neck as in a choir

We could be interpreted as white sponge-paint blobs
    on light-blue walls

and we climb from floor to top of wall, then wrap
    around the ceiling

Surely our people will arrive; we should hear footsteps
    on the staircase in the hallway

We wait for the family reunion we've been dreaming of—
    a tumble of youngsters, elders, cousins

A cacophony of footsteps begins. Children calling,
    parents whispering about what they'll find

Will they be thrilled, comforted, or terrified to see
    us specters? Shall we fade or stand strong?

Ghosts of the dead, we are in our bodies, but
      not in this world

They don't need to see us, but they do need to feel
      our presence

And the living arrive. Young Daniel starts to sing
      in clear tones,

Power from whom all blessings flow; connect us
      with the Gone we know . . .

The room is suffused with vibration; sound waves
      bound up the ceiling

and circle our heads, allow us to stretch our
      flimsy limbs. They know we are

not demons, we are spirits reaching down with hearts
      and open arms

Nightmares of former occupants who permeated our walls
      disappear

Perhaps after the reunion ends, new tenants will choose
      wallpaper with peaceful images

Gulls flying high over the horizon, another layer
      of palimpsest, capable of transparent contact

With relief we can return behind this scrim, knowing
      there is no death, only otherworldly hope

Benjamin

She bids us wait,

wait for messages

from beyond the Veil. Wait.

All hands on the table, we sit for rotation.

After time, it wobbles,

tilts and turns.

A levitating trumpet

helps Anna Lee amplify

voices as yet unheard.

Before long, the temperature drops,

lights flash on and off,

a soft red glow remains around

the tall tarnished candlestick,

beads on the lampshade tremble.

We hear insistent rapping

at the far wall,

louder, louder.

Spines prickle, adrenaline flows

through the tops of our hands,

and Anna Lee calls out

Benjamin?

Mrs. Blanchette's face pales,

her shoulders twitch,

as her elder son, a Civil War casualty,

murmurs in the darkness:

Fret not, Mama, my brother was spared

this time.

He describes bloody

leaves on the fields at Chancellorsville,

bodies dismembered, intestines bared,

his own breastbone shattered,

head severed.

The trumpet, still in flotation,

accompanies Anna Lee

in conjuring Benjamin,

compounding their voices.

Fear not, Mama, we will

be to . . . ge . . . ther . . . a . . . non . . .

His voice fades,

hers rustles away.

We let Benjamin go,

holding hands and swaying

in unison,

all hands on the table.

Past Life

Research by Dr. Jim Tucker, University of Virginia, and
other renowned physicians suggests that similar accounts
from other two- to six-year-olds are credible.

Mama, I used to be someone else.

Ricky has a jagged purple birthmark on his right forearm,
and a larger one just below the ribs on the left side of his back.
At four years old, he says he was a movie star,
and danced on stage in Hollywood in the twenties.

My real name was Morris Pulowski.

He insists, he cajoles—he describes pin-sharp details
as if he were an adult:

> *I worked in a talent agency when I got older,*
> *I was an actor before that.*
> *I had a big house with a pool*
> *My street address started with an "M,"*
> *maybe Mulholland?*

> *Am I the only person who lived before?*

Mama, studying reincarnation and plowing
through old Hollywood movie photos,
shows Ricky picture after picture:

> *Hey Mama, that's Gregory.*
> *We did a film together.*

His finger shot over to a man in the photo wearing a
trench coat and a frown.

> *And that's me. I found me!*

Police records and newspaper articles from Los Angeles
relate a story about a man found dead
at a movie studio in that era.

As Pulowski left the Paramount lot, a stranger advanced,
a trigger clicked.

Was the shooter a paramour of a female star on the set?
Was there a love triangle?

Photos of the victim show the gun shot entered
Pulowski's right forearm and the bullet expanded,
exiting his back on the left side—

Mama, I used to be someone else.

What to Expect at Congressional Cemetery

Not the graves that drew me there
Not the closed iron gates where I found a side opening
Not the numbered maps leading to celebrity headstones

I tuned to the un-named, the no ones, the un-knowns

Confused by the totem poles along the brick walk
Distracted by the verse I was waiting for
Bewildered by grief and loss and heat

I blinked through sweat, turned my straw hat upward

Curious about the K-9 dog-walkers
who paid to be in the special society of cemetery donors—
we were all deciphering Washington DC anew

Not the St. Albans where my first husband taught
Not the Van Ness building where I lived for twenty-eight years
Not the Eastern Market flat I rented during separation

I tuned to hundreds of years of burying

The 1892 epitaphs from husband to wives
Tipped-back headstones of proud gay lovers
Locked vaults saved for self-claimed venerables

I fled back to the totems, the red carved cedars

      The female bear of liberty
      Male eagle of war
      Turtle in the middle of the crossbar

I learned comfort from carver Jewel Praying
Wolf James from Lummi Nation, Washington state
This is the verse I was waiting for:

Mother Earth holding us up
Father Sun covering us down
Animals watching over us

All our arms are linked underground
wrapped around one another, our crooked
feet all know pain and suffering

Postcards Way Over the Edge

When I saw the postmark on your letter
I knew you were having a great time!
You *did* grow younger, Dad.
Your hips no longer cause stabbing pain.
You're playing awesome rounds of golf,
often par, which you don't hesitate to point out to friends.
Still drinking tons of whiskey and soda,
and your doctor claims your heart is stronger than ever.
You maintain perfect weight, in fact as you swear that
chocolate cake does more for the soul
than damage to the gumpa.
You've become best friends with your brother again,
he moved from Methuen to be near you a few years ago.
Impassioned speeches about politics keep you going,
early absentee voting is the way you'll back Kamala.
You say you'll try your hand at poetry, "it's easier,"
and you've had enough of oils and turpentine for a while.
Mom's breaking all records as a broker, started her own firm
with her brother who moved from Pittsburgh to be near her.
Both your cars, *The Pimp* and *The Shrimp* are running well.
Mom loves her blue leather seats, yours smell a bit fishy.
The bucket of worms dried up, but hell,
you'll use it as mulch for your asparagus garden.
You say the weather is just about perfect, you give
strangers rides on clouds in your electric cart, they love the view.
Please beam me down your street address so I can reply—
all I have on your note is Elysian Fields, zip code 00000

Climbing the Rohtang Pass

Barely twelve, I understood how daunting the climb:
Rohtang Pass, Himachal Pradesh, border of India.

Elevation—thirteen thousand, a three-day ascent—
Stay-over at two base camps, canvas tents, oolong tea.

Small trekking party with mules and supplies; practiced
sherpas scanning for snow, deadly landslides.

Difficult terrain to the south, Kullu Valley, forests of deodar;
rocky rubble to the north, Spiti Valley, jagged peaks.

Throughout the years, those who chanced the crossing
learned that Rohtang Pass meant "Pile of Corpses."

The Gods' Mountain jealously guarded that name;
human beings attempting to change it were met with silence.

Dad's photo of me when I reached the Pass, stretching
out prone on top—corduroy pants, woolly jacket, Tibetan cap.

I felt airborne into China, hovering over mounds of ice.
Perhaps those frozen souls below had chosen to stay there.

The rush of wind, vast endless view could drown us all—
a sensation of snow under our bellies for the rest of time.

Benumbed

It can get dark on the mountain
A faint sun without hope disappears
You are surrounded by silence

Hollow trees have already
wrapped their arms around
themselves

A slash of thin leaves provides
no home for the lone bear
who circles the frozen ground

Rare flashes from stars reflect
birds frozen mid-air, iced
by stinging winds

A moose with heavy antlers
backs away from the lake
Dead otters line the creek

Determined spiders crawl slowly
up your torso to pull
your eyelids shut

A dull ache cups your ears
The band tightens around your head
It can get dark on the mountain

Trees Have Longer Lives

I know the voluminous Hemlock on my mountain

will always know more than I.

Tall, erect, it once stood alongside young hedges

that since surrendered.

Over years, the giant sent long roots below—

not to harm anything, only to stand strong.

Many trees huddle midst families;

this one remains alone.

What we pass fleetingly, the wizened one protects:

boisterous bickering of blue jays and squirrels;

black bear with brown muzzles

growing fur for the season;

Siberius Iris, bursting perfume through raindrops;

overjoyed children, galloping with laughter;

sad conversations between lovers no longer.

The Hemlock absorbs all life's events;

attacks endured, sun saluted, sorrows sustained.

Its supple trunk carries the load,

leaves clapping their memories.

I hope never to witness rings or scars,

but to revel in its graceful branches

reaching ever higher, blowing us messages—

for my revered tree will have longer thoughts

than we, and longer longings.

Fillilulu

My dad was certainly not a scientist, nor accurate
    in his animal-fact reporting, but he had grace and humor.

He used to read me fantasies, like *Alice in Wonderland*,
    and made up his own stories about bats and mice.

He probably talked to visiting wildlife in New Hampshire;
    I know he left notes for squirrels at the back door.

On a road trip he once asked me, "How do deer know
    they shouldn't cross at the Moose X-ING?"

Intrigued when he told me that "fillilulu" birds fly backwards;
    I was pretty sure he meant hummingbirds,

but I googled "fillilulu" birds to see what I could find.
    Nothing at all, so I dug into hummingbirds—

Scientists note these are nectar-sipping beauties,
    whirring from flower to flower with agility and grace.

With long beaks, like hydraulic pumps, they eat beetles, aphids
    and mosquitoes, and love sugared-liquids in feeders.

They recognize bird-lovers who create the treat. Over time,
    they let these humans come near, even perch on their fingers.

Many cultures consider hummingbirds, "Spirit Animals."
    Around the world, people view them as healers

and messengers to deceased ancestors. If they appear to you
    in person or in a dream, it is a sacred event,

evidence that you are connected with other souls
    on the astral plane.

When my father was fast failing, I remembered something
    comforting he had told me years ago in college—

I was floundering in Astronomy, upset I would fail,
    but he said, "Don't worry, your stars are in the right place."

I wonder what he would have thought of my dream of metallic—
    bronze and gold fields, acres of glowing wheat,

vibrating wings hovering above, specs of ruby-red
    and shimmering sapphire—mighty little birds.

I think he would have been quite sure that whether fillilulus or
    hummingbirds, they brought enchantment and wonder,

an air of magic. In hospice, the night before he died, the doctor
    told him, "Not much time." Dad replied, Elysian Fields.

My sisters and I hovered around, like hummingbirds,
    hearts beating twelve hundred times per minute.

If I could have told him the birds in the dream were singing
    wordless songs, I bet he would have said,

They can't talk back to you, but their friends will understand.
    And, the truth as far as fillilulus go—

they do fly backwards and upside-down.

Buteo

"He's looking for someone to kill," said the couple
who pulled alongside me on the road.
I was mesmerized by the turkey-sized bird who goaded,
glared at me, warned trouble.

"His beak says raptor," as they watched from their safe car.
Standing near the broad field,
I turned stiff as a statue.

How still he was, assured of his presidency,
his royal residence, his acres of mixed-grass greenery,
his sky-high tree not so far away.

Yet like a dog when primed for attack,
his odd ruff stood up, not on his black-feathered back,
but puffing out from long-shank bird legs—

a swelling like flared dandelion fluff.

And then, in his surety, off!

What had seemed a leaden earth-bound body,
bright yellow and white markings,
now was on airstream—
riding wild current, flaming red tail fanned.

How he soared, then hovered in one place,
looking for his rabbit.
At that moment I was a mouse-sized mammal,
prayerful prey.

We are all raptor and prey,
but he is sure of what he is doing.
I knelt to his gesture.

Mighty Red-tailed Hawk

Beyond Beauty

At dusk,
a muster of peafowl
gathers in the courtyard—
peahens perch high above in khejri trees,
peacocks strut along pathways below,
lined with beds of golden dew-drops
and hibiscus flowers.
We marvel
at what seems to be a regal mating game,
fascinated as we watch
from the polished
marble patio of the Oberoi Hotel in Jaipur.

The males rattle their shimmering
emerald green feathers,
emitting low-frequency sounds,
twenty-six times a second.
Sensors in the female crests attune
perfectly to these vibrations—
one willing peahen shakes,
vibrates in unison,
and descends from her look-out.

She chooses the bird with the showiest fan,
the most teal ocelli, his oval eyespots,
and advances.
The peacock mounts her,
aligns his abdominal opening with hers,
sends in his seed.
And then he moves on.
National bird of India,
he proceeds with dignity
and assurance.
Picking up his four-toed feet
in a syncopated strut,

he surveys his premises,
overlooks his territory.

Captured by his brilliant color,
the striking iridescence,
we are blinded, yet compelled, like her.
The peahen doesn't just see his iconic fan,
she feels him in her head.

Peacocks signal miracles can happen,
shedding their plumage
every year after mating season.
A peacock knows it's never too late
to come alive again, regrowing
a train of greater glory and splendor—
a resurrection, almost a reincarnation.
His message rattles forward:
Embrace your beauty,
show off your gifts,
heal once more.

Riptide Swimmer

Any fool can get into the ocean. But it takes a Goddess to get out.
—poet Jack Spicer

From the shore to the moon, upward winds
drag small shells along the ocean floor
twirling the jet streams that keep swirling
in spirals, and blindly ascending
to disappear in black holes and sentries of stars
Limpid algae melts in the undertow

I am a clam, soft and tender—
amorphic, gathering calcium from shells
of dead relatives in the terrigenous sediment
to build my own protective tent
When safe, I push to shore in the swell and ebb,
mingling with flotsam and seaweed

I am remade—
in the beach sand, I am Something—
Nothing but quartz and feldspar

The Bug I Cannot Name

Last evening, I stepped onto the balcony—

hot, moist.

From there, I could hear a million birds

calling in abbreviated phrases.

A bug, beetle-shaped but with wings,

buzzed by the web of my curly hair.

It menaced, warned, repeated:

> You are not here for long
> not on this balcony
> not in this univerzzz.

All birds ceased song.
One I could spot in the slippery elm tree
turned his orange beak my way,
open mouth waiting.

The bug dive-bombed again.
Armed with black rubber swatter,
I slammed it against the deck rail.
It would have been better
if Orange-Beak had swallowed it.

No one was there to judge me or comment.

I walked inside,
pushed the screen door shut, thinking:

When I am gone,
will the northern cardinals
open their beaks waiting,

or call
wheep,
wheep,
wheep?

Orca Ode

Inspired by "The 17th Day," a short story by Christina Cogswell, telling that seventy-five percent of orca calves died in the Salish Sea, Puget Sound, in 2018, due to PCBs from shipyards, manufacturing, slaughter houses, and Superfund clean-up sites.

The world always
begins in the ocean,
in many seas around the globe,
as moonlight moves across water.
Tahlequah, resident orca J-35, swam
for seventeen days in the Salish Sea,
pushing her dead newborn.
She would not let her baby's body,
400 pounds heavy, sink.
Breathing for Tahlequah
was a conscious act—
She had to come
to the surface for air
every twelve minutes—
She nosed her
daughter's limp body
upward with her.
This was a "Tour of Grief,"
but she did not go it alone.
For millions of years,
orcas have lived
in matrilineal pods,
with an elder female guiding.
A group of five or six
surrounded her.
Not the only one
to push the body,
they all took turns.
On the seventeenth day,
Tahlequah dropped the baby,
went to the top for air.

She let her calf be reclaimed
by the sea's blue womb,
let it drift away.
The rest stayed with her
at the surface,
dipping and rising in mourning.
A tightknit group,
they circled in harmony,
directly centered in a moonbeam,
even as it moved across the waves.

At the Retreat, Esalen

It's late and darkness falls, but still my eyes are keen,
I peer for baby seals in the blackness of the sea.

My room, high upstairs, three windows wide open,
invites in the crashing echoes of waves. I stare

through the shadows and crooked tree branches
to find bobbing heads in the surf—

Swirls of water around rocks have a rhythm,
I wait for white splash-ups to subside.

Odd that the space between heads stays consistent,
none dive under the surface—

Not a single black skull crashes into the cliffs,
in fact, swimmers in clusters seem to hold hands.

Aha! Tiny topknots are kelp bulbs sloshing in concert,
safely anchored below—all sea plants, not pinnipeds!

I ruminate as I close the windows,
Where in the black night do daytime seals go?

Elephas Maximus

Matthew, my keeper, thinks he knows me:
he reports that unlike most females who gather in groups,
I choose to stand by the water hole alone

    swaying side to side

Some might say I'm shifting my five-ton body to be
more comfortable, but I know the baby-bull inside
could take twenty months to emerge

    swaying inside me, all two hundred pounds of him

Matthew prepares three hundred pounds of food a day
for me—grass, tree bark, fruit, stems, and hay—
bananas and jackfruit

he thinks I'm smart, very smart—
recognizing myself in mirrors like dolphins and chimps—
recognizing all the keepers who take good care of me,

    who say that I sway side to side for stimulation

Matthew says the motion keeps me cool, and that I'm
a good swimmer, seeing that I have a
permanent snorkel, thanks to my trunk

He invites visitors to guess my age, by
the telltale pink spots on my trunk and
patches on my flapping ears

He's loyal and affectionate, spending hours making
me push logs and roll tires for exercise,
chopping carrots and sugarcane that I love

Matthew knows that at night, I can lie down sideways but
during daytime nap hour, can choose to stand,
perhaps in a state of readiness to move on

Here is what Matthew cannot know:
what I hide inside my brain— memories of my mother,
the matriarch, who led us across the savannah—

remembering how she taught us to bathe everyday
spraying up water until completely clean,
then spraying sand all over our hides so

no sunburn could reach us, no insects could infest;
She showed us how to swat away
pests with the hairy loop of her tail

A newcomer to captivity, I retain memories of how
I used my sense of smell to find year-old dried dung,
left by my mother near the grave where her herd

            buried her—a dart in her side

I sway because I could not pluck
the deathly needle from her lumbering
body, spray dust in the wound

These are just dreams now, distant visions.
I embrace my zoo quarters far from Gujarat,
with other orphans who could not survive alone

When I blink my long eyelashes, the keepers who toil
to know us, think it is to keep bees from stinging,
but Matthew may know it is to hide my tears

            I sway,
and for him, my favorite, I stop to wrap my trunk
gently around his bony ankles

Chelonia

Maybe I think I really am a turtle
Sometimes I feel I hold the world upon my back
how indulgent that sounds, or worse, just dumb

Maybe I think my body is my temple
I swim, I walk, I row, I lift, I collapse:
this is hardly spiritual; it's simply physical

Maybe I am a late bloomer because I'm learning
to move slowly; otherwise, I bruise easily
I thought I had a thick skin, a shell, but no

it's just I tend to duck and cover. I'm getting
more sensitive: I say no to social events,
hide out and binge television series of love and loss

Maybe I was born to battle, not to succumb;
turtles proceed with intention; they know they can
beat the frantic hare, serve as a model

and so, I look back over centuries and sing my turtle praise to you,
Spirit Turtle:

>   You, O Chelonia, eponymous
>   holding the world upon your back
>   are recognized on earth as prophetess
>
>   Wrongly seen for slothfulness
>   you merely need to retreat and retract
>   You, O Chelonia, eponymous
>
>   With patience and balance—if ponderous—
>   You stay intent, remain on track
>   So many on earth see prophetess

Your shell and bones astonish us
especially your kin, the Leatherback
You, O Chelonia, eponymous

For tranquility, you gain prominence
For fertility, like an almanac on track
Souls on earth see you as prophetess

Wise and steadfast symbol, you promise us
longevity, and through eons, impact
O Chelonia, turtle eponymous
You are blessed on earth as prophetess

Reconsidering the Moon

We think you continue to change, but oceans know better.
Moon, you keep your same face towards us, a constant truth.

At *new*, we are close to each other, nocturnal animals
scamper to the shadows, badgers mate.

Your waxing crescent, a lemon slice, sneaks a peek,
waiting for the *first quarter* to test appearances.

At full, Australian corals release massive eggs and sperm,
doodlebugs make bigger traps for active prey.

You hide nothing, proud to show your bruises and welts.
Ungainly as you go *gibbous*, losing faith,

losing confidence, aware that the *third quarter* will
offer a stillness, time for stable reflection.

Waning crescent sweeps away all regrets, while lions attack
and kill. Scorpions grow blue in your moonlight.

Ever the Full Moon

Quarter, wax, wane—mysterious one—

easy to forget you are always there,

though the oceans keen so closely.

Shadow, shadow—new, so darkly fetal,

dimmed to keep your secrets,

while night creatures await your sly peek.

Revolve, revolve—absolve your early hide-out,

be proud of your half-full glow,

like yellow Venetian glass, you reflect a smile.

Oh gibbous, how ungainly!

You have rubbed your edges jagged,

like youth, aching for muscle beauty.

Shine, shine, now shiny ornament!

You are naked full-face forward,

by force your loud cheeks burn

hot, too hot—now fold to wane,

show your uneven hide,

shadows melting on the other side.

You glance again, and bend

to face backward, to slide around the arc

of darkness. You hear fast footsteps

following, as you arrive once more at new.

You have not gone by, nor ever will,

until the sun burns away to cosmic dust.

Five Seasons (Ode)

Virginia Woolf wrote, " ... we change fact by force of imagination,"

and hence I conjured Everywhen:

a heavy additive to Winter, Spring, Summer, Fall, ready when

the extra nakedness of late Fall comes—a kind of starvation—

Our dread of shorter days, a numbness, a sedation;

harvests have well departed; gray wolves plump their fur.

Greeks see the coming of late Fall as the sadness of Demeter,

her kidnapped daughter trapped in isolation.

Like Everywhen, a holding pen of death before the snow;

fuscous bark of trees dry hard and plants stop making food.

Birds migrate fast on flyways—fierce mallards on the move;

a beech tree clings to dusky leaves that clutch and curl in shadow—

I rustle up the truth of barren Everywhen, especially when

winter is not so future, cruel ice its deadly sin.

Late February

Morning came and it was tight and chalky

More snow throughout the night, iced over

Fir fingers droop downward, saddened by gravity

Low bushes, once red, crouch beside gray clapboard walls

Twigs, that yesterday pressed out tender shoots and buds,

crack and shrivel

Tender leaves curl, and clench their fists

Casualties of winter

Mercury Goes Retrograde

Mercury retrograde describes a time period that comes three or four times a year when Mercury, the planet of communication, appears to be moving backwards in its orbit. In truth, it's an optical illusion.

—Astrologist Constance Stellas

While Mercury Retrograde has become known as a dreaded messenger of mix-ups, miscommunication, and madness, we firmly believe that when we align ourselves with the energy of the universe instead of fighting it, life will always be in harmonious flow.

—Anonymous

Three times a year, Mercury goes retrograde
All goes wonky, time for reassessment
What happens to communication?
Mercury speeds by earth, kicking up dust,
which disrupts my body, makes me feel rushed
and fills my brain with odd vibrations
Fallout is widespread and really annoying
My habits and machines all need upgrades

I lose my balance, need considerable first aid,
forget appointments, make poor investments
Mess up relations, try explanations
Dishwasher dies, this is really unjust—
Scads of emails get lost—to my utter disgust
Mercury! Come back for a consultation
Tell me *slow down; re-do, be observant;*
choose calm and kindness; make anger fade

Remember that life can be a crazy parade
Doctors dare to go into retirement
Old friends choose to move across the nation
Parking tickets blow off in a gust

dumb GPS fails; a fender gets crushed
Just chill—this is a passing situation
Buy pink silk pajamas, a sound investment,
Wear a personal crystal, preferably jade

Farewell to Glorious Pink at the Basin

—inspired by Gerard Manley Hopkins

Praise the blossoms of spring with *Hosanna!*
Westerly, breezily, wafting, and sensuous.
Sing to all the unknown and most glorious.
Yesterday, cherry trees fluttered me on,
today, all dampened, a slant rain fell down.
A million delicate confettis loosen
pinkish-gray lace on the carpeting, brown.
Onlookers, who once paraded, are gone.

But all for this! A duck glides by—
tourmaline, shimmering, confident trail.
Trees watch, they neither mourn, nor sigh.
Seasons do rise, some withered oak will fail.
But orange tulips push into the sky—
Chorus of ripples and branches chant *Hail!*

Shades of Anger

—after reading about color theory by Johann Wolfgang von Goethe
and Joseph Albers

Broad brushstrokes of rage are red,
streaked by dark brown doomsday dread,
But, mine hold peaks of bluish darts,
emerging from black where hatred starts

Tints of Anguish

My paintbrush turns tan into blurred arcs of soot,
underscores grief that knots in my gut.
Braided shapes tighten to clot in the center,
burnt tan loneliness moans in surrender.

Serenity Hues

I thought I knew what serenity was without color:

a meditation of repeating murmurs;

low chants from the monastery on the hill;

muffled Tibetan bells traveling the valley.

But then I see the sap green lily pad, pushing

from an under wash of umber muck and gray stems,

surrounded by endless ripples of dusky ultramarine.

A fragile lotus flower bursts forth:

its seedpod heart of cadmium yellow tickled

by stringy strands of peach, wriggling bean sprouts;

its crown ringed by petals, reaching up like candlelight flames;

pale pools of lavender, thin stripes of whisper white

tipped in violet.

The Healer

—after Nancy Josephson's sculpture *The Healer*

A multicolor-beaded rabbit figure sniffs her forearm,

seeming to know the healer holds cures in the vials

of lavender, rosemary and ashwagandha seeds

that hang all around her head, neck, bust and arms.

She faces forward, resolutely, solemnly—

bold white eyes in her black sculptured head,

tightly beaded, ringed with rounded rhinestones.

Perfect gold eyebrows match the two

striations on each cheek, markings of honor.

The rabbit sniffs again, forepaws surround

her upper torso in protection or prayer,

stiff cotton tail, stark-still.

The air suggests they both are in a moment

of meditation or recalibration—for the healer

has eons of restorative mending yet to do.

Her left eye starts to emit a golden glow as her head

tilts up toward a distant sun, beyond all

earthly places where she brings compassion

and psychic elixir to eager souls.

Rabbit knows her mystery magic and

remains silent near her glowing moss green

waist, waiting for a visitation—

innumerable supplicants advance.

The Time-Markers

—as told by artist Nancy Josephson of *Flow-Through,
The Time-Markers*, busts built during the COVID
pandemic to represent her emotional landscapes

Like Damballa in the pantheon of Vodou spirits,

I start the pandemic in March 2000 in hope.

Building my bust of beads and tangle of snakes

in a snood, I think the confinement will only be two weeks.

Although my whitened face is slightly red,

my orderly breastplate of tiny white beads

and high-necked rhinestone choker imply serenity:

Two more weeks, two more weeks.

Months go by, and now I am the Fire-Starter,

furious that our leaders trade power for compassion.

I construct a fierce bust of black beads,

a wild spray of golden dreadlock hair,

topped with three candles that glow angrily.

Hot wax drips from smaller clumps of candles on my shoulders,

a sharp sword-like triangle on my neck suggests murder:

I want to kill, I want to kill.

Two years pass, I am coming to New Light,

humbled, transformed, but still not calmed.

My face an opaque white, small fissures track

down my temples to my ears. My hair,

a heightened helmet of bead strings underlit

by blue-white mini-bulbs. My mouth and bust silenced

by netting, I dub myself "Caul." Infant, crone, priestess:

Wait, watch, Wait, watch.

Dactylic Halloween Ditty

—in praise of spells, amulets, and grace

Now is the witches' famed New Year

Veil to the lifeless most thin

Tools to be gathered, spells murmured low

Bygone truths whispered by kin

Don't leave your shoes upside down

or mix orange mangoes with milk

Never put purses on floorboards

nor pass in the pathway of owls

Please summon spirits and angels

Phantoms who speak in the wind

Harken to laws of the wiccan

Hear how we chant in a coven

Dance under moonlight with branches

Rattle your shells, seeds and berries

Welcome the ghosts

who wander through crowds

Drop little beads of blue moonstone

Charm folk with gift sacs of amulets

Warn them when someone's behind

Float back and forth within time

Witch Tree at Sweetbriar

She's a mushroom-shaped tree

formed by skinny branches

trailing to the ground—

long grey-brown strings

with bumps at the knuckles

and pointed fingernails.

They cross over each other

in the breeze forming

momentary cat's cradles,

the largest of the limbs

dotted with bare age spots.

A single branch sticks out the top,

its birdlike beak open—

a plea to the cobalt sky above.

Tender shoots of new branches

emerge at her feet,

baby witches-in-waiting,

turning green.

Our spirit-witch hides

behind a large invisible

blue bubble during the day,

watching over the next generation

through her lifeless boughs.

The crone is tired at her core.

Her trunk, like an elephantine hulk,

droops as her many legs fold in lumps.

The ones that spill to the ground host

dry wells of crushed plants and flowers—

cinnamon, lime, mugwart, myrrh.

Our elder, the healer,

prepares to sink to the underworld.

Tarot Sonnet: New Love

Tarot cards insist "Your time is now!"

We never had the chance before.

Bright Star sings, "high time to explore."

Two of Cups infers, "go ahead," somehow.

Page of Pentacles asks, "Is this the life you want anyhow?"

Old partners fall away, we hear The Tower roar,

"Your moment of truth explodes, your freedom, furthermore."

Returning magnets, we circle back to allow

that I will beckon, you will offer fragrant flowers.

We tread lightly at first, avoid tilting too far.

We take advice from Temperance, Lion, and Justice,

whose silent strength bring wisdom that empowers

us to heed joy, hunt bliss, shun obstacles that bar.

As final blessing, the High Priestess whispers, "Trust us."

Passiflora Incarnata

A rondel of pale lavender petals stopped me
Layers of color popped from green leaves below
I sent him a photo not knowing the name
marveling at multiple layers of whorls

Layers of color popped out from green leaves
He made a pastel drawing based on my photo
marveling at the layers of frond and whorls
wiggly sprouts of violet, stars of lime green

He kept the photo and finished the sketch
and sent it dated February 14
Eye-catching sprouts turned violet to green
Five-pointed star topped with white stalks

The drawing reached me on Valentine's Day
I framed it, but packed it away for a time
those eye-catching purples surrounded by green
Not knowing the genus, I named it Wild Lily

Later, he arrived and unpacked the drawing
hung it on my wall among colorful artworks
Not knowing the meaning, I called it Wild Lily
and blossomed like her amidst his soft colors

All through the rooms among dazzling artworks
we were a case of laughter and passion
blooming, unfolding and flaming with embers
Oblivious of names for what to call this life

We were a wild case of laughter and passion
having lived a long time, having reveled in color
Now, searching for names to understand this gift
we found that the flower was really a vine

Having lived a long time, having had many plants
It was clear the flower was alluring but tough
We learned it was not just one bloom, but a vine
growing like wildfire from summer to fall

This winsome flower was alluring but tough
thought to mean hardy ambition in life
growing like wildfire from summer to fall
I discovered its formal name in 2023

Latin for ambition and optimism in life
Passiflora incarnata sounded so carnal
I discovered that formal name in 2023
matching the photo, the drawing, our love

Passiflora incarnata is luscious and sensual
The floret shows up and wants quick attention
matching his drawing, our short time together
I searched for the science of the sweet blooms

"Passion-Flower" certainly required attention
matching our love, its wild intertwining growth
But botany about its growing season and blooms
brought forth facts, a deep structure was missing

"Passiflora is known for wild growth,
succeeding best when supported by a wall"

Love's armature was missing—*"the growth season*
long, but blooms never last for more than one day"

Spirits

Call me Hecate, I travel by night,
my broom casting spells upon men.
They wonder why I must take flight.

Compare me to fleet Aphrodite,
crooning love songs as she ascends.
Call me Hecate, I travel by night.

to conjure new schemes I raise to incite,
aware that the change I require offends.
Small wonder that I must take flight.

Antigone warns by sharing foresight
how women can stand unrepentant.
Call me Hecate, I travel by night.

Explore! rebel! To create is my right.
I need warriors, willing kings to attend,
not wonder why I must take flight.

Harken the wild man, the lover and knight
who pushes me higher, delights in my pen.
Call me Hecate, I travel by night,
as darkness descends, I bloom and take flight.

Excursion (Ars Poetica Odyssey)

With no dress on, I (she/her) walk into town.
I have no idea if anyone will be there, nor
do I know if I can find a Mom and Pop
Coffee shop, or if Tom the Drycleaner is reliable.

There's something pleasant about watching
for upturned sidewalk slabs, pushed up
by enormous tree roots bursting below,
causing a hop in my step.

I notice that the hardware store is old-fashioned,
cobbler's bench in the front window,
metal cabinet with small drawers for loose screws
against the back wall.

I admire the vibrant Coca Cola logo,
cursive red letters, those beautiful scripted "C's,"
and wonder out loud, "Do vendors in this
town have a Convivial Community Convention?"

Continuing in fall sunshine, mostly I come up
with words about how warmth feels on bare shoulders.
Tangerines in the outside bins of the grocery store
are fragrant, bookstores flaunt their indie status.

I gather my lines that halt at the crosswalk,
syllables slip into Brandy's Winery.
Next door I discover demitasse at Café Olay,
and sink into the Queen Anne chair.

Leaning on a faded velvet armrest of doilies, I
look around for metaphor, find croissants
cruising for apple jelly, lemon cookies vying
for raw sugar frosting, a ½ & ½ carton yawning.

Perhaps the baker will appear with a surprise,
an anthology? I hazard a guess that
I am invisible since no one notices when I
raise my extra-long fingers to write

a message on the tin ceiling squares: "Ode."
Rain begins a staccato rhythm, then pelts.
I'm starting to think my narrative works,
it's time to bring the odyssey on home.

Fifty Senses

While aware of sight and sound, smell and touch,

    and the well-known sense of taste—

Through time, I have felt there must be more, and

O, the bliss to count again, not only the five,

    but more than ten—

the bitch of itch and soreness of too-dry-skin

the notion of motion, when balance fails

a recognition of hormonal shifts while kissing

feelings through intense recall, premonitions of hereafters

It's not just that I'm old, I wager, or have the words

    to describe keen body knowledge; it's

just that I sense other ways of knowing:

the nuzzle and flick, the fumble and grip,

fast shock of electromagnetic fields, neck hair rising,

the surety that someone is behind me

It's more about—an innate knowledge of direction,

     the expectation of stretch, expanding, contracting,

perception of pain—skin thinness, nerve-endings.

Simultaneous translation goes on between body

and emotion: itch becomes irritation with someone;

loss of balance or making mistakes heralds inner conflict,

not necessarily dementia.

I know the rhythm of day and night, my orientation

     of up or down,

an eerie gut sense of telepathy and clairvoyance.

I believe sensations beyond my limbs,

I experience joy of silent

songs in my sleep—unheard shouts within nightmares.

     I swim in space,

     and this I know:

I must be a faun, or leprechaun;

maybe a Djinn, or psychic, a skeptic

blended with enthusiastic spiritualist,

or, indeed, a sensual crone—

Certainly, a witch

When in Doubt, Channel Bob Marley

—inspired by Bob Marley's song "Three Little Birds"

unh cheh cheh,   unh cheh
unh cheh cheh   unh cheh

The "I'm-not-ready dream"
    I was having
        portended big disaster

All folding chairs were
    lined up in the hallway. Why
        were they not in place?

My guests looked expectant
    standing at the door
        waiting to be cared for

I planned to feed them—hot
    curry in pink ceramic
        bowls. Was it ready?

The alarm clock I set last night to give
    me time to prepare
        jolts me awake. What now?

A song I know wafts
    through my haze
        and words begin to form:

Don't worry . . . 'bout a thing

Hey wait, I'm supposed to
    perform, and I'm not
        dressed!

The computer glares at me,
         screen saver blinking
                  printer disconnected

Where are my copies, the playlist,
         the intros? I can't find my
                  mic, or my podium

Spontaneously, the tune returns:

Don't worry...'bout a thing

People arrive, the birds fly inside—
         efficient chambermaids
                  aligning chairs, seating guests

Chattering cheerily, they offer champagne
         Napkins draped over royal-blue feathers,
                  they pass pink bowls of curry

The microphone is set and actually working
         and I am ready, I even
                  have my gold shoes on

The clapping begins,
         the guests join the chorus,
                  my Rasta birds keep time:

unh cheh cheh,   unh cheh
unh cheh cheh   unh cheh

A Guitar, A Woman

—inspired by B. B. King's career, his beloved guitar, and legacy

B. B. passed in his sleep that May,
sad day, two thousand fifteen.
Up very late the night before,
he paid homage to his queen

Back at the Club on Beale Street,
he built a shrine with care.
The shape of his favorite "axe" Lucille,
formed the back of every chair.

Every seat downstairs
was shaped like his guitar—
an ode to his best lady,
she'd carried him so far.

Mourners at his gravesite,
heavy heads cast down,
sang midnight blues with sorrow,
drank whiskey through till dawn.

Customers on Beale Street
now lounge on wooden chairs.
The sound of his soulmate, Lucille,
alongside trumpets flares.

She backs up souls and bodies
while brass and keyboards ring.
They know that she's electric,
there's tension in gut strings.

Rest your torso on her body,
tilt your head against the frets,
she'll bend the sounds as blue notes,
he'll wail off favorite riffs.

Lucille and B. B. linger
through songs that stand supreme.
Her chairs as shrines and his
sweet soul charm fans in Tennessee.

Higher Spirits, Better Selves

—with utter admiration for E. B. White, author of *Charlotte's Web*

Some Pig
Terrific
Radiant
Humble

"We are dealing with supernatural forces here,"
proclaimed the judge at the county fair

"Humans must always be on the watch for the coming of wonders,"
preached the small-town minister

"We are born, we live a little, we die,"
taught Charlotte A. Cavatica, gray spider
in the barnyard of animals

And Wilbur the Pig, who loved her as his best friend,
rose to the occasion that she prescribed—Believe in yourself!

But first, he cried
And then, he explored
After that, he enjoyed:
      gamboling of sheep
      idio-idio-idiosyncrasies of geese
      yummy beechnuts, truffles, and roots
      whippoorwilling of birds in tall trees
      winning "A Famous Pig" prize

He even turned backflips, while smiling

Yet sometimes, he cried, wailed, and fainted with fear;
in fact, he talked about his travails:
      with Fern, who bottle-fed him in infancy
      with Templeton the Rat, who tried but failed to be a

villain, and Charlotte, who saved his life
but told him she would die after childbirth

Mysteries prevail, miracles happen:

Men change their mind about
killing weaker creatures such as litter runts;
514 baby spiders get born, spin their own silk;
love their godfather pig, and leave home

Life goes on—

Astonishing,
Glorious,
Heart-Rending

Grasping for Faith, A Ballad

—after studying the Old and New Testaments during the pandemic

Almighty, please explain pestilence—
What has been wrought on the world?
Oceans turn bloody, frogs disappear,
insects are swarming, hail stones unfurled.

Moses, remember old Egypt—
Locusts descended, foul stenches arose.
Boils festered, first-borns were slain,
Someone marked blood above doors.

John, it's written you baptized
a teacher who roamed far afield—
this miracle worker turned wonders,
but strangely asked aides to conceal

his identity as The Messiah—
Why hide it if it were true?
Gospel scribes proved humans are vile,
even three-in-one Gods can abuse.

Holy Ghost, when did you enter?
Did the world need more than Two?
Fathers and Sons are mystery enough.
Why a Trinity? Names can confuse.

Back to the present, I wonder
is COVID the start of more plagues?
Apocalypse followed by Judgment?
Believers have waited for ages.

Perhaps other Spirits have answers,
like songs of bold gremlins and imps.
Come Fairies! Devilkins! Goodys!
Bring scriptures to offer a glimpse

of hope for a future less gloomy,
strong leaders who won't desecrate.
Let them wander the globe spreading truth,
letting science and divers faith conflate.

Allow all beliefs to be heralded,
Exclusions would be a sore loss—
Read from the Qur'an, Upanishads,
Testaments, Pantheon of Myths.

Be humble, pay attention to Nature,
take heed of the meaning of Host.
Recognize lepers and paupers—
Embrace obscure Gods and veiled ghosts.

A Billion Big Bangs

There was a time when we thought the world was flat.

Look! A New Universe—the Huge Surprise
Look at the spiral-armed deep star flanging,
planets once unseen. Galaxy clusters, up to now
dim blobs, burst into multicolor exclamations!
Sadly, our earthly state is darker, despite a
starry Milky Way—human beings are hissing,
Texas children missing, nuclear threats in the offing,
nationwide shootings appalling.
We drown in Kansas floods and tornadoes,
witness bloated whales on syringe-strewn beaches;
watch mangroves shrivel from oil-leak breaches.
O, Pray for visions beyond black holes. Conjure
unimaginable new frontiers,
curtains of color dancing across new skies.
Wonder at wavelengths,
heed the star-gazers who probe cosmic depths with hope—
They,
who see thirteen billion light years away.

Rags

Kantha, which means "old rags" in Sanskrit, was created
years ago by Bengali women in India

Since Vedic times, old saris, piled in layers, are
basted together in strong but rough-shorn blankets

bonded in a running stitch. Passed on through generations
for warmth and protection, they are infused with family lore

Kantha quilts hold a certain magic—enveloping prayers,
vows, stories—given to children, cousins, people in need;

sometimes tied to wave from trees or draped on shrines,
all assembled in good faith by women

A present came my way, tiny kantha balls strung
as a necklace

Shades of orange, gold, brown—pressed into rounds,
sewn in running stitch by hand

Tradition holds, yet this time made by a young woman
born in Kyushu, schooled in fashion design in Tokyo,

raised in North Carolina. Inspired and intrigued by
the spiritual nature of transforming old rags,

she creates new art by reincarnating saris from distant lands
in novel forms with grace and respect

❖ ❖ ❖

She is borrowing beauty, honoring tradition,
slowly choosing worn-out cloth—

folding and shaping, pressing and shrinking.
She strings beads, wavy and soft, for hours and hours

to keep her wearers safe from harm by preparing
amulets for their necks—

Seekers and creators, peering across time and space,
sharing stories, stitched in history

Notes

[20] "Ghosts of the Dead," inspired by Marvin Cone's *The Appointed Room*;
https://www.pinterest.com/pin/391602130081592986

[60] "The Healer," after Nancy Josephson's sculpture *The Healer*;
https://www.nancyjosephsonart.com/sared-gallery/spirit-heads/#bwg13/224

[62] "The Time-Markers," as told by artist Nancy Josephson of *Flow Through—The Time-Markers*, busts built during the COVID pandemic to represent her emotional landscapes;
https://www.nancyjosephsonart.com

About the Author

LEE WOODMAN is the author of the "Scapes" poetry series and winner of 2023 IPA, Independent Press Award, for Distinguished Favorite in Poetry. She is also winner of the 2020 William Meredith Prize for Poetry, the 2021 Atlantic Review International Poetry Competition Merit Award, and First Prize in Poetry and Prose Contest for *Carve Magazine* 2022. Her essays and poems have been published in *Tiferet Journal, Zócalo Public Square, Grey Sparrow Press, The Ekphrastic Review, vox poetica, The New Guard Review, The Concord Monitor, The Hill Rag, Naugatuck River Review,* and *The Broadkill Review.* A Pushcart nominee, she received an Individual Poetry Fellowship from the DC Commission on the Arts and Humanities FY 2019 and FY 2020, and a Virginia Center for the Creative Arts Fellowship in March 2022. Her poetry collection, *Mindscapes,* was published by Poets' Choice Publishing in 2020, *Homescapes* in 2020 by Finishing Line Press, *Lifescapes* by Kelsay Books in 2021 and *Artscapes* by Shanti Arts in 2022. Woodman has been a featured guest on numerous radio shows and podcasts, including *The Authors Show, Goodnews Broadcasting, Ron Van Dam, Steve Maggi, Cyrus Webb,* and *Cover to Cover Book Beat with Roger Nichols.*